CHARLIE PARKER
FOR BASS

20 Heads & Sax Solos
Arranged for
Electric Bass with Tab

Cover Photo by Michael Ochs Archives/Getty Images

ISBN 978-1-4803-8513-9

HAL•LEONARD®
CORPORATION
7777 W. BLUEMOUND RD. P.O. BOX 13819 MILWAUKEE, WI 53213

Visit Hal Leonard Online at
www.halleonard.com

FROM *Summit Meeting at Birdland*

Anthropology

By Charlie Parker and Dizzy Gillespie

Solo

7

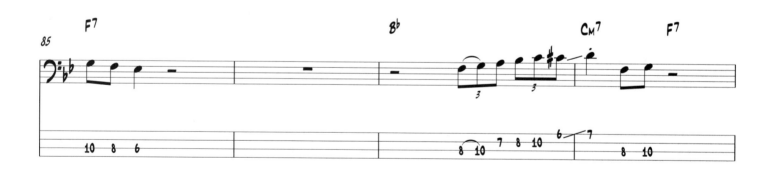

8

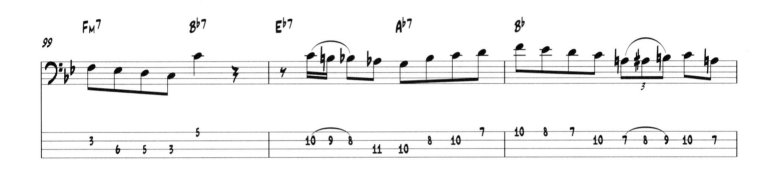

FROM *BIRD'S BEST BOP ON VERVE*

Au Privave

By Charlie Parker

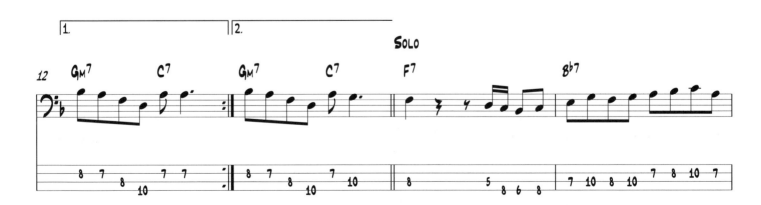

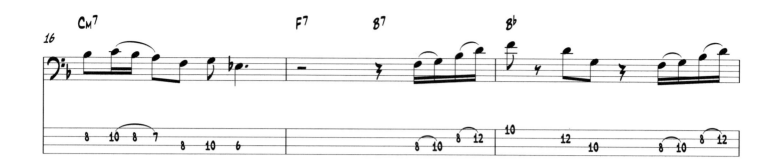

13

From *The Complete Savoy & Dial Master Takes*

BILLIE'S BOUNCE
(BILL'S BOUNCE)
By Charlie Parker

SOLO

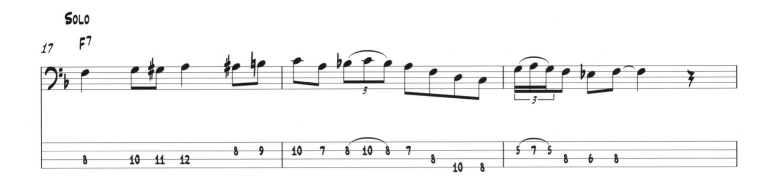

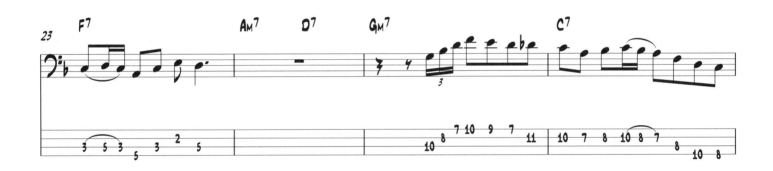

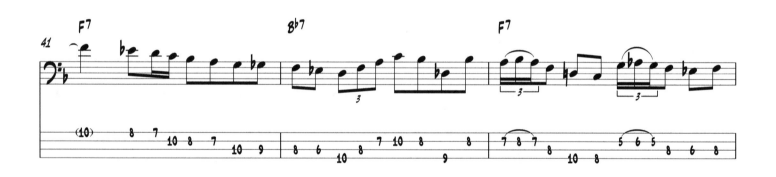

*Played behind the beat.

FROM *The Essential Charlie Parker*

Bloomdido

By Charlie Parker

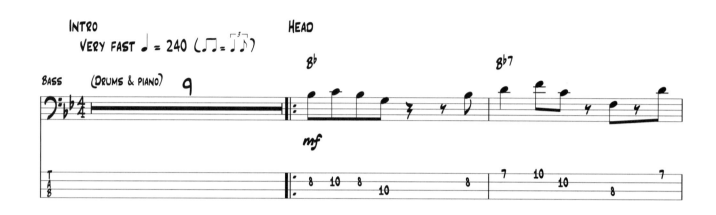

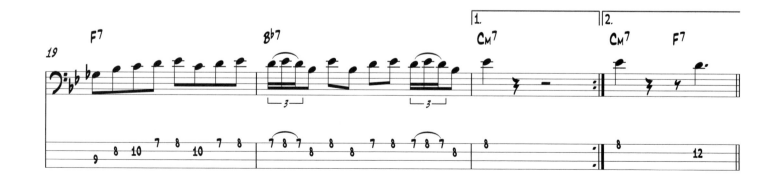

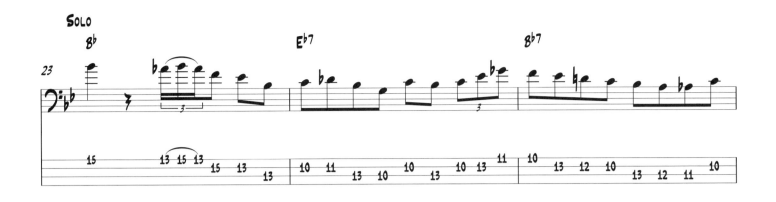

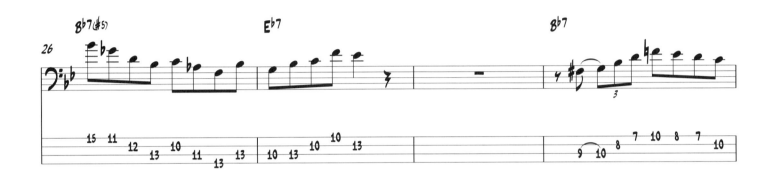

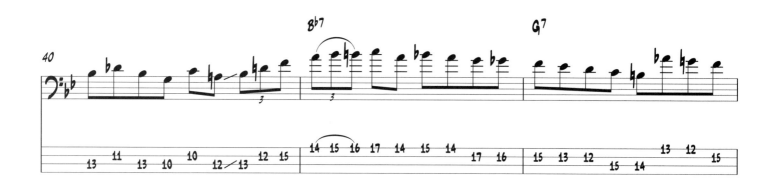

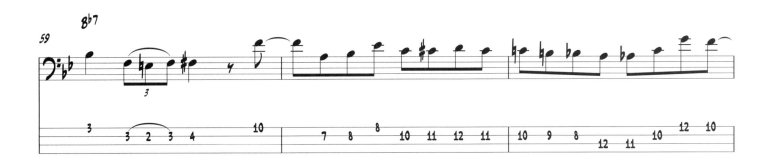

Blues For Alice

By Charlie Parker

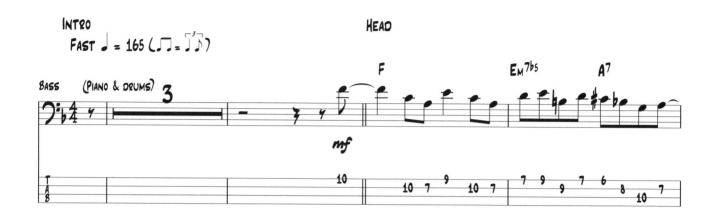

FROM *Bird: The Complete Charlie Parker on Verve*

Chi Chi

By Charlie Parker

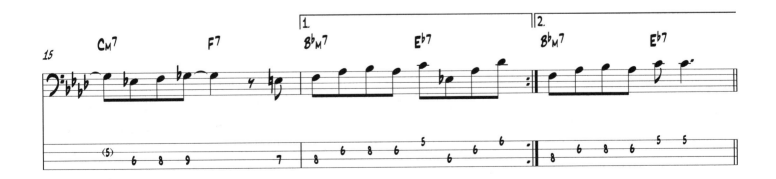

from *The Essential Charlie Parker*

Confirmation

By Charlie Parker

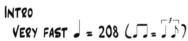
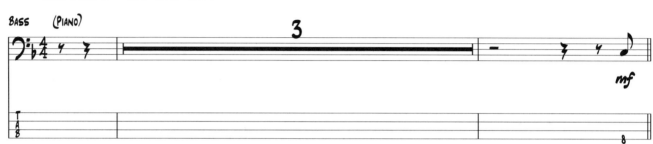

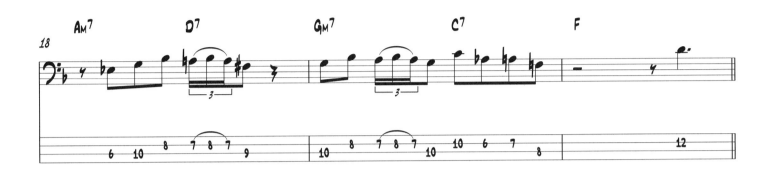

from *The Complete Savoy & Dial Master Takes*

Dexterity
By Charlie Parker

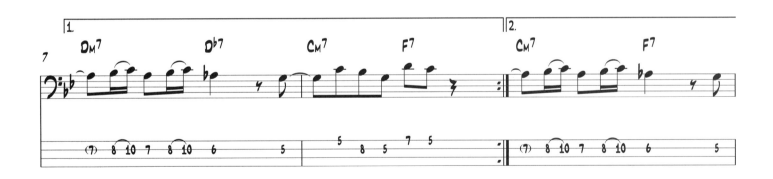

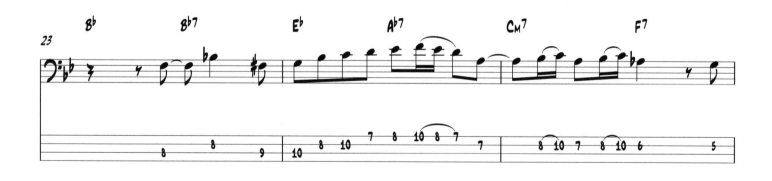

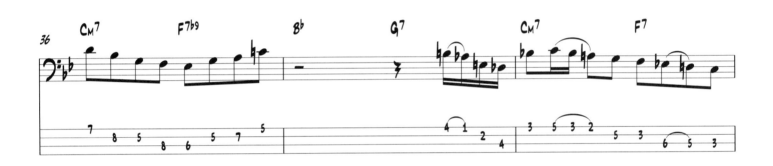

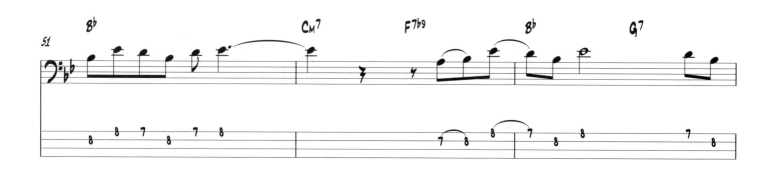

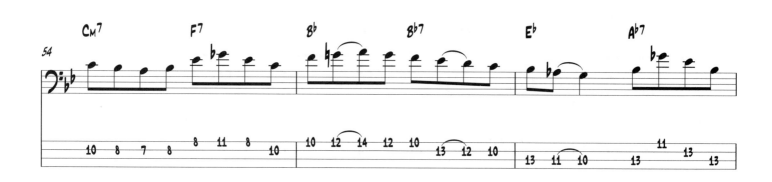

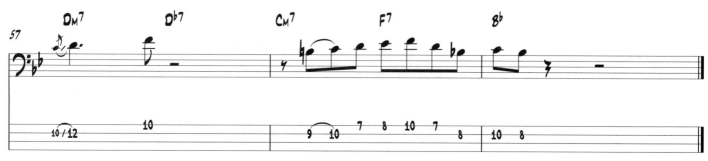

FROM *The Complete Savoy & Dial Master Takes*

Donna Lee

By Charlie Parker

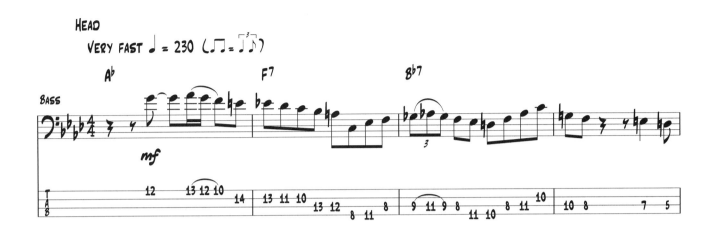

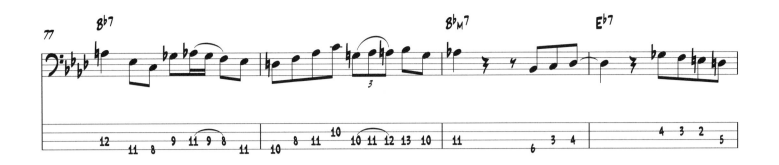

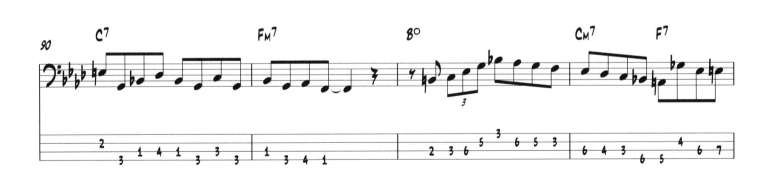

FROM *The Essential Charlie Parker*

K.C. Blues

BY CHARLIE PARKER

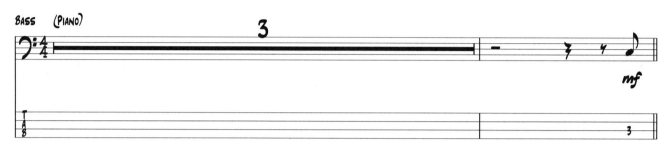

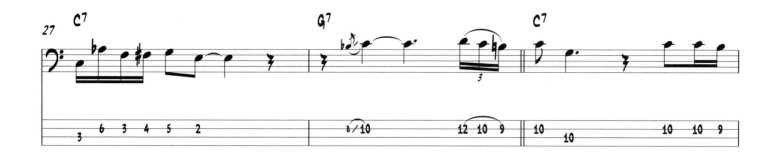

*Played behind the beat.

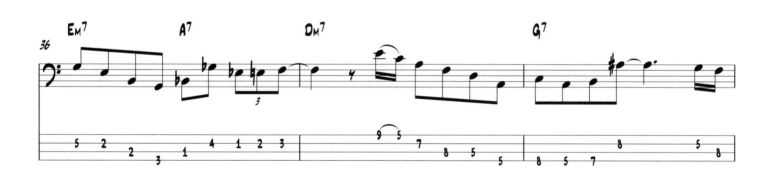

FROM *The Complete Savoy & Dial Master Takes*

Ko Ko

BY CHARLIE PARKER

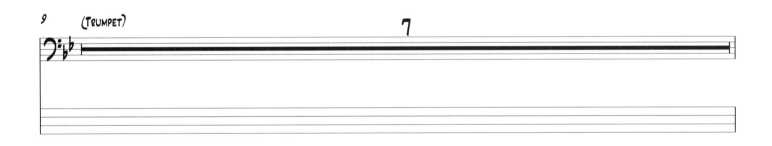

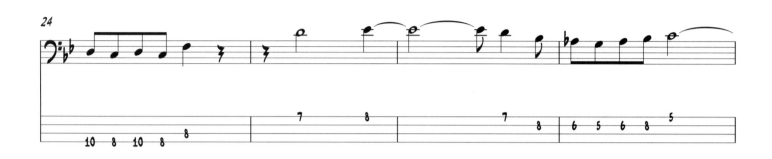

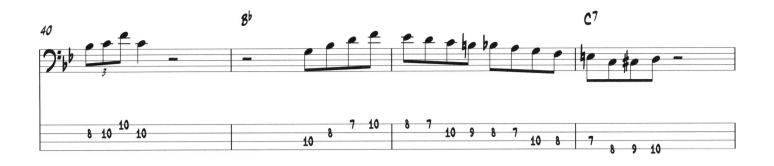

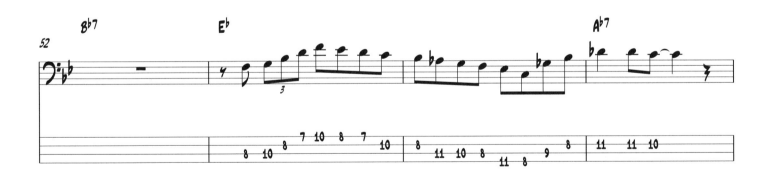

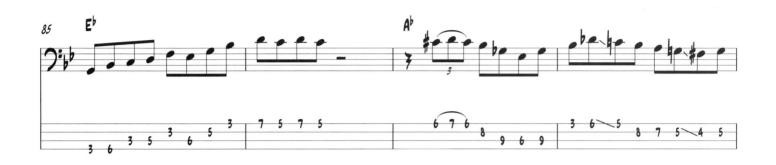

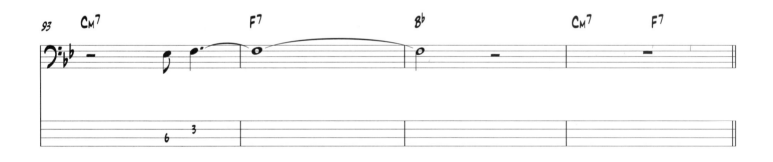

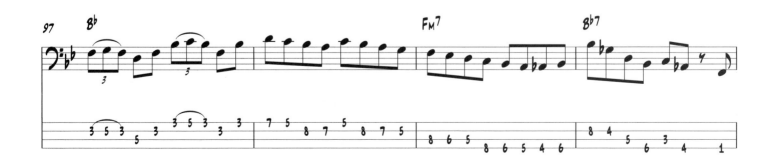

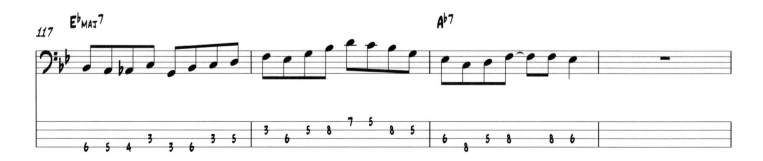

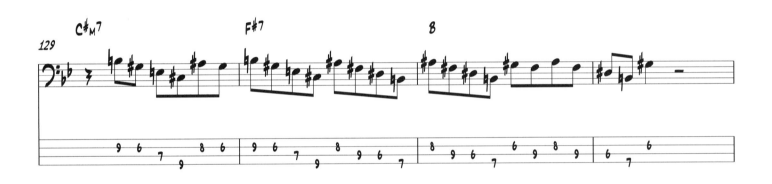

FROM *The Complete Savoy & Dial Master Takes*

Moose the Mooche

By Charlie Parker

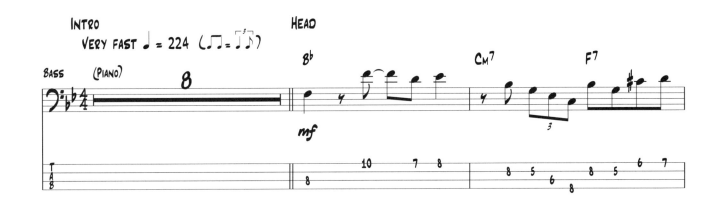

My Little Suede Shoes

By Charlie Parker

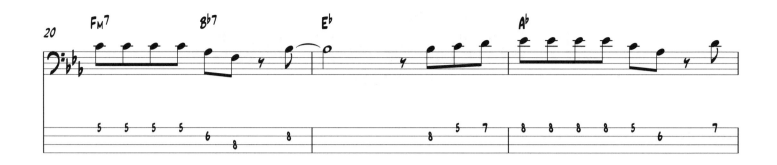

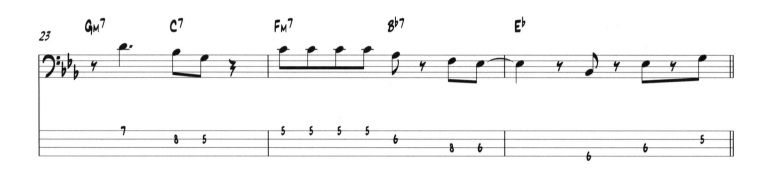

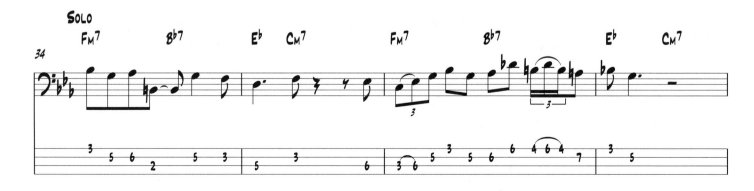

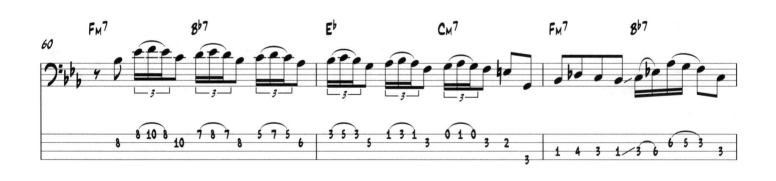

FROM *The Best of Charlie Parker 20th Century Masters*

Now's the Time

By Charlie Parker

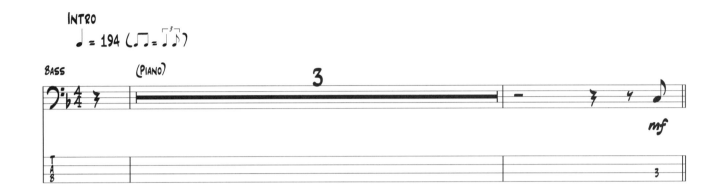

SOLO

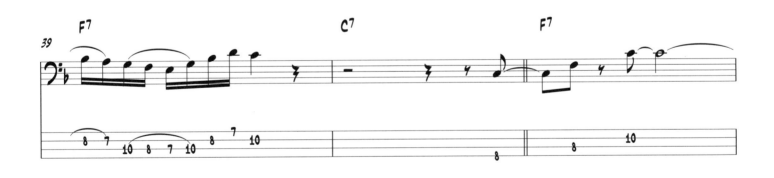

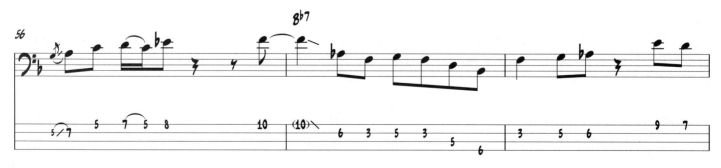

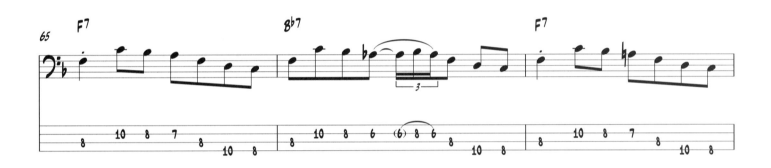

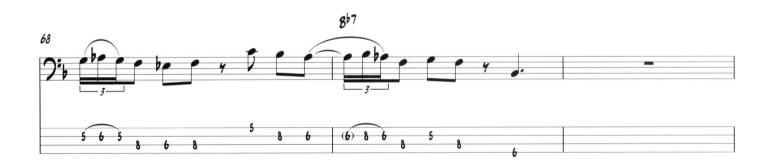

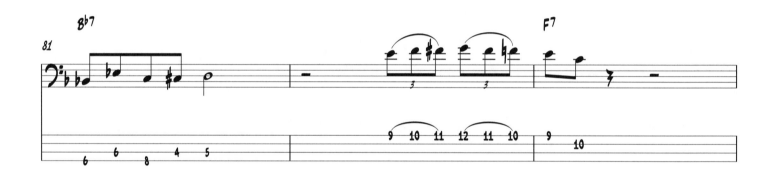

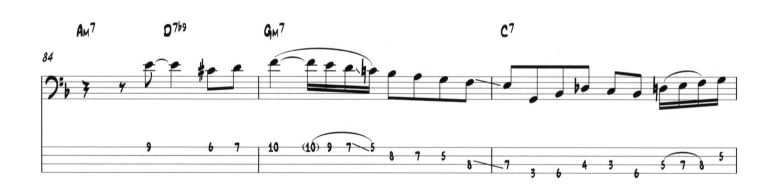

FROM *The Complete Savoy & Dial Master Takes*

Ornithology

By Charlie Parker and Bennie Harris

FROM *The Complete Savoy & Dial Master Takes*

Parker's Mood

By Charlie Parker

FROM *The Complete Savoy & Dial Master Takes*

Relaxin' at the Camarillo

By Charlie Parker

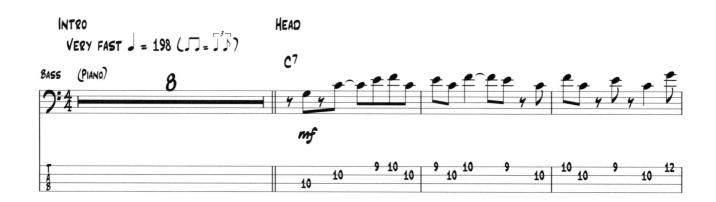

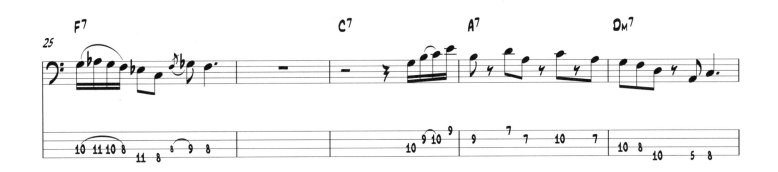

FROM *The Complete Savoy & Dial Master Takes*

Scrapple From The Apple

By Charlie Parker

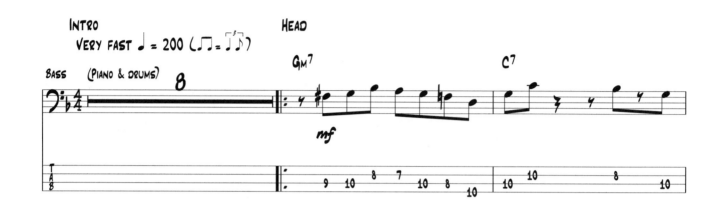

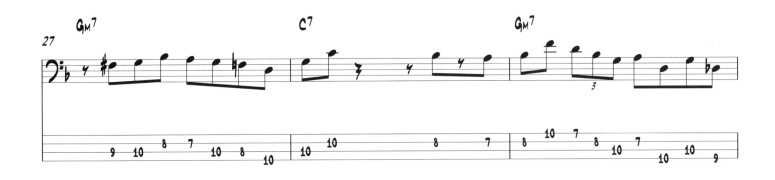

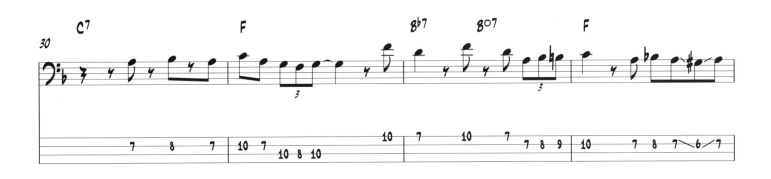

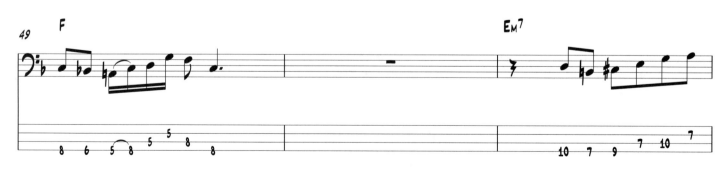

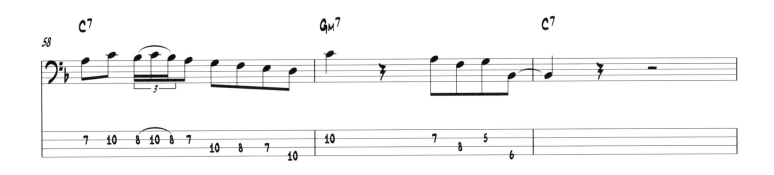

from *The Complete Savoy & Dial Master Takes*

Thriving from a Riff

By Charlie Parker

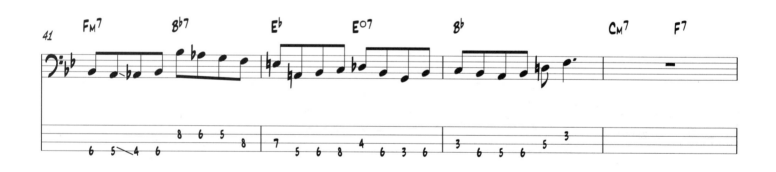

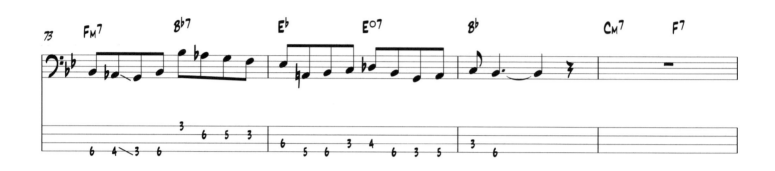

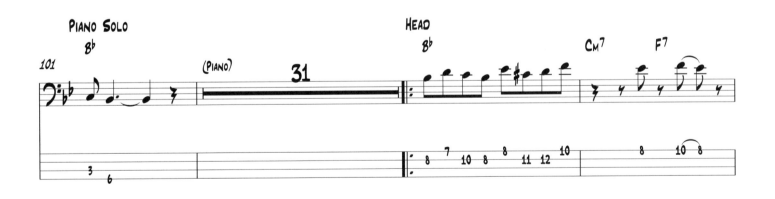

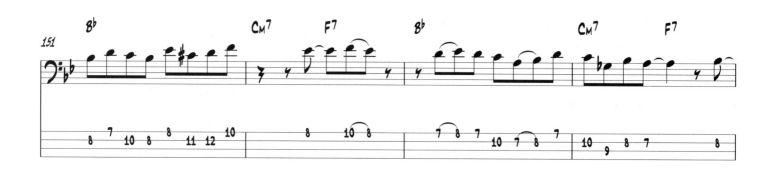

FROM *The Complete Savoy & Dial Master Takes*

Yardbird Suite

By Charlie Parker

BASS NOTATION LEGEND

Bass music can be notated two different ways: on a *musical staff*, and in *tablature*.

THE MUSICAL STAFF shows pitches and rhythms and is divided by bar lines into measures. Pitches are named after the first seven letters of the alphabet.

TABLATURE graphically represents the bass fingerboard. Each horizontal line represents a string, and each number represents a fret.

3rd string, open   2nd string, 2nd fret   1st & 2nd strings open, played together

HAMMER-ON: Strike the first (lower) note with one finger, then sound the higher note (on the same string) with another finger by fretting it without picking.

PULL-OFF: Place both fingers on the notes to be sounded. Strike the first note and without picking, pull the finger off to sound the second (lower) note.

LEGATO SLIDE: Strike the first note and then slide the same fret-hand finger up or down to the second note. The second note is not struck.

SHIFT SLIDE: Same as legato slide, except the second note is struck.

TRILL: Very rapidly alternate between the notes indicated by continuously hammering on and pulling off.

TREMOLO PICKING: The note is picked as rapidly and continuously as possible.

VIBRATO: The string is vibrated by rapidly bending and releasing the note with the fretting hand.

SHAKE: Using one finger, rapidly alternate between two notes on one string by sliding either a half-step above or below.

NATURAL HARMONIC: Strike the note while the fret hand lightly touches the string directly over the fret indicated.

MUFFLED STRINGS: A percussive sound is produced by laying the fret hand across the string(s) without depressing them and striking them with the pick hand.

BEND: Strike the note and bend up the interval shown.

BEND AND RELEASE: Strike the note and bend up as indicated, then release back to the original note. Only the first note is struck.

RIGHT-HAND TAP: Hammer ("tap") the fret indicated with the "pick-hand" index or middle finger and pull off to the note fretted by the fret hand.

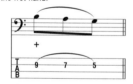

LEFT-HAND TAP: Hammer ("tap") the fret indicated with the "fret-hand" index or middle finger.

SLAP: Strike ("slap") string with right-hand thumb.

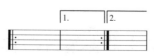

POP: Snap ("pop") string with right-hand index or middle finger.

Additional Musical Definitions

(accent)	•	Accentuate note (play it louder).
(accent)	•	Accentuate note with great intensity.
(staccato)	•	Play the note short.
	•	Downstroke
V	•	Upstroke

D.S. al Coda   • Go back to the sign (𝄋), then play until the measure marked "**To Coda**," then skip to the section labelled "**Coda**."

D.C. al Fine   • Go back to the beginning of the song and play until the measure marked "***Fine***" (end).

Bass Fig.   • Label used to recall a recurring pattern.

Fill   • Label used to identify a brief melodic figure which is to be inserted into the arrangement.

tacet   • Instrument is silent (drops out).

• Repeat measures between signs.

• When a repeated section has different endings, play the first ending only the first time and the second ending only the second time.

NOTE: Tablature numbers in parentheses mean:
     1. The note is being sustained over a system (note in standard notation is tied), or
     2. The note is sustained, but a new articulation (such as a hammer-on, pull-off, slide or vibrato) begins.

The Best-Selling Jazz Book of All Time Is Now Legal!

The Real Books are the most popular jazz books of all time. Since the 1970s, musicians have trusted these volumes to get them through every gig, night after night. The problem is that the books were illegally produced and distributed, without any regard to copyright law, or royalties paid to the composers who created these musical masterpieces.

Hal Leonard is very proud to present the first legitimate and legal editions of these books ever produced. You won't even notice the difference, other than all the notorious errors being fixed: the covers and typeface look the same, the song lists are nearly identical, and the price for our edition is even cheaper than the originals!

Every conscientious musician will appreciate that these books are now produced accurately and ethically, benefitting the songwriters that we owe for some of the greatest tunes of all time!

VOLUME 1

00240221	C Edition	$35.00
00240224	B♭ Edition	$35.00
00240225	E♭ Edition	$35.00
00240226	Bass Clef Edition	$35.00
00240292	C Edition 6 x 9	$30.00
00240339	B♭ Edition 6 x 9	$30.00
00451087	C Edition on CD-ROM	$25.00
00240302	A-D CD Backing Tracks	$24.99
00240303	E-J CD Backing Tracks	$24.95
00240304	L-R CD Backing Tracks	$24.95
00240305	S-Z CD Backing Tracks	$24.99
00110604	Book/USB Flash Drive Backing Tracks Pack	$79.99
00110599	USB Flash Drive Only	$50.00

VOLUME 2

00240222	C Edition	$35.50
00240227	B♭ Edition	$35.00
00240228	E♭ Edition	$35.00
00240229	Bass Clef Edition	$35.00
00240293	C Edition 6 x 9	$30.00
00451088	C Edition on CD-ROM	$27.99
00240351	A-D CD Backing Tracks	$24.99
00240352	E-I CD Backing Tracks	$24.99
00240353	J-R CD Backing Tracks	$24.99
00240354	S-Z CD Backing Tracks	$24.99

VOLUME 3

00240233	C Edition	$35.00
00240284	B♭ Edition	$35.00
00240285	E♭ Edition	$35.00
00240286	Bass Clef Edition	$35.00
00240338	C Edition 6 x 9	$30.00
00451089	C Edition on CD-ROM	$29.99

VOLUME 4

00240296	C Edition	$35.00
00103348	B♭ Edition	$35.00
00103349	E♭ Edition	$35.00
00103350	Bass Clef Edition	$35.00

VOLUME 5

00240349	C Edition	$35.00

Also available:

00240264	The Real Blues Book	$34.99
00310910	The Real Bluegrass Book	$29.99
00240137	Miles Davis Real Book	$19.95
00240355	The Real Dixieland Book	$29.99
00240235	The Duke Ellington Real Book	$19.99
00240348	The Real Latin Book	$35.00
00240358	The Charlie Parker Real Book	$19.99
00240331	The Bud Powell Real Book	$19.99
00240313	The Real Rock Book	$35.00
00240323	The Real Rock Book – Vol. 2	$35.00
00240359	The Real Tab Book – Vol. 1	$32.50
00240317	The Real Worship Book	$29.99

THE REAL CHRISTMAS BOOK

00240306	C Edition	$29.99
00240345	B♭ Edition	$29.99
00240346	E♭ Edition	$29.99
00240347	Bass Clef Edition	$29.99
00240431	A-G CD Backing Tracks	$24.99
00240432	H-M CD Backing Tracks	$24.99
00240433	N-Y CD Backing Tracks	$24.99

THE REAL VOCAL BOOK

00240230	Volume 1 High Voice	$35.00
00240307	Volume 1 Low Voice	$35.00
00240231	Volume 2 High Voice	$35.00
00240308	Volume 2 Low Voice	$35.00
00240391	Volume 3 High Voice	$35.00
00240392	Volume 3 Low Voice	$35.00

THE REAL BOOK – STAFF PAPER

00240327		$10.99

HOW TO PLAY FROM A REAL BOOK

FOR ALL MUSICIANS
by Robert Rawlins

00312097	$17.50

Complete song lists online at www.halleonard.com

Prices, content, and availability subject to change without notice.

HAL•LEONARD® CORPORATION

7777 W. BLUEMOUND RD. P.O. BOX 13819 MILWAUKEE, WI 53213

1113

73. **JAZZ/BLUES**
00843075.....................$14.95

74. **BEST JAZZ CLASSICS**
00843076.....................$15.99

75. **PAUL DESMOND**
00843077.....................$16.99

76. **BROADWAY JAZZ BALLADS**
00843078.....................$15.99

77. **JAZZ ON BROADWAY**
00843079.....................$15.99

78. **STEELY DAN**
00843070.....................$15.99

79. **MILES DAVIS CLASSICS**
00843081.....................$15.99

80. **JIMI HENDRIX**
00843083.....................$16.99

81. **FRANK SINATRA – CLASSICS**
00843084.....................$15.99

82. **FRANK SINATRA – STANDARDS**
00843085.....................$16.99

83. **ANDREW LLOYD WEBBER**
00843104.....................$14.95

84. **BOSSA NOVA CLASSICS**
00843105.....................$14.95

85. **MOTOWN HITS**
00843109.....................$14.95

86. **BENNY GOODMAN**
00843110.....................$15.99

87. **DIXIELAND**
00843111.....................$16.99

88. **DUKE ELLINGTON FAVORITES**
00843112.....................$14.95

89. **IRVING BERLIN FAVORITES**
00843113.....................$14.95

90. **THELONIOUS MONK CLASSICS**
00841262.....................$16.99

91. **THELONIOUS MONK FAVORITES**
00841263.....................$16.99

92. **LEONARD BERNSTEIN**
00450134.....................$15.99

93. **DISNEY FAVORITES**
00843142.....................$14.99

94. **RAY**
00843143.....................$14.99

95. **JAZZ AT THE LOUNGE**
00843144.....................$14.99

96. **LATIN JAZZ STANDARDS**
00843145.....................$15.99

97. **MAYBE I'M AMAZED***
00843148.....................$15.99

98. **DAVE FRISHBERG**
00843149.....................$15.99

99. **SWINGING STANDARDS**
00843150.....................$14.99

100. **LOUIS ARMSTRONG**
00740423.....................$16.99

101. **BUD POWELL**
00843152.....................$14.99

102. **JAZZ POP**
00843153.....................$15.99

103. **ON GREEN DOLPHIN STREET & OTHER JAZZ CLASSICS**
00843154.....................$14.99

104. **ELTON JOHN**
00843155.....................$14.99

105. **SOULFUL JAZZ**
00843151.....................$15.99

106. **SLO' JAZZ**
00843117.....................$14.99

107. **MOTOWN CLASSICS**
00843116.....................$14.99

108. **JAZZ WALTZ**
00843159.....................$15.99

109. **OSCAR PETERSON**
00843160.....................$16.99

110. **JUST STANDARDS**
00843161.....................$15.99

111. **COOL CHRISTMAS**
00843162.....................$15.99

112. **PAQUITO D'RIVERA – LATIN JAZZ***
48020662.....................$16.99

113. **PAQUITO D'RIVERA – BRAZILIAN JAZZ***
48020663.....................$19.99

114. **MODERN JAZZ QUARTET FAVORITES**
00843163.....................$15.99

115. **THE SOUND OF MUSIC**
00843164.....................$15.99

116. **JACO PASTORIUS**
00843165.....................$15.99

117. **ANTONIO CARLOS JOBIM – MORE HITS**
00843166.....................$15.99

118. **BIG JAZZ STANDARDS COLLECTION**
00843167.....................$27.50

119. **JELLY ROLL MORTON**
00843168.....................$15.99

120. **J.S. BACH**
00843169.....................$15.99

121. **DJANGO REINHARDT**
00843170.....................$15.99

122. **PAUL SIMON**
00843182.....................$16.99

123. **BACHARACH & DAVID**
00843185.....................$15.99

124. **JAZZ-ROCK HORN HITS**
00843186.....................$15.99

126. **COUNT BASIE CLASSICS**
00843157.....................$15.99

127. **CHUCK MANGIONE**
00843188.....................$15.99

128. **VOCAL STANDARDS (LOW VOICE)**
00843189.....................$15.99

129. **VOCAL STANDARDS (HIGH VOICE)**
00843190.....................$15.99

130. **VOCAL JAZZ (LOW VOICE)**
00843191.....................$15.99

131. **VOCAL JAZZ (HIGH VOICE)**
00843192.....................$15.99

132. **STAN GETZ ESSENTIALS**
00843193.....................$15.99

133. **STAN GETZ FAVORITES**
00843194.....................$15.99

134. **NURSERY RHYMES***
00843196.....................$17.99

135. **JEFF BECK**
00843197.....................$15.99

136. **NAT ADDERLEY**
00843198.....................$15.99

137. **WES MONTGOMERY**
00843199.....................$15.99

138. **FREDDIE HUBBARD**
00843200.....................$15.99

139. **JULIAN "CANNONBALL" ADDERLEY**
00843201.....................$15.99

140. **JOE ZAWINUL**
00843202.....................$15.99

141. **BILL EVANS STANDARDS**
00843156.....................$15.99

142. **CHARLIE PARKER GEMS**
00843222.....................$15.99

143. **JUST THE BLUES**
00843223.....................$15.99

144. **LEE MORGAN**
00843229.....................$15.99

145. **COUNTRY STANDARDS**
00843230.....................$15.99

146. **RAMSEY LEWIS**
00843231.....................$15.99

147. **SAMBA**
00843232.....................$15.99

150. **JAZZ IMPROV BASICS**
00843195.....................$19.99

151. **MODERN JAZZ QUARTET CLASSICS**
00843209.....................$15.99

152. **J.J. JOHNSON**
00843210.....................$15.99

154. **HENRY MANCINI**
00843213.....................$14.99

155. **SMOOTH JAZZ CLASSICS**
00843215.....................$15.99

156. **THELONIOUS MONK – EARLY GEMS**
00843216.....................$15.99

157. **HYMNS**
00843217.....................$15.99

158. **JAZZ COVERS ROCK**
00843219.....................$15.99

159. **MOZART**
00843220.....................$15.99

160. **GEORGE SHEARING**
14041531.....................$16.99

161. **DAVE BRUBECK**
14041556.....................$16.99

162. **BIG CHRISTMAS COLLECTION**
00843221.....................$24.99

164. **HERB ALPERT**
14041775.....................$16.99

165. **GEORGE BENSON**
00843240.....................$16.99

167. **JOHNNY MANDEL**
00103642.....................$16.99

168. **TADD DAMERON**
00103663.....................$15.99

169. **BEST JAZZ STANDARDS**
00109249.....................$19.99

170. **ULTIMATE JAZZ STANDARDS**
00109250.....................$19.99

172. **POP STANDARDS**
00111669.....................$15.99

174. **TIN PAN ALLEY**
00119125.....................$15.99

175. **TANGO**
00119836.....................$15.99

176. **JOHNNY MERCER**
00119838.....................$15.99

***These CDs do not include split tracks.

Jazz Instruction & Improvisation

BOOKS FOR ALL INSTRUMENTS FROM HAL LEONARD

AN APPROACH TO JAZZ IMPROVISATION
by Dave Pozzi
Musicians Institute Press
Explore the styles of Charlie Parker, Sonny Rollins, Bud Powell and others with this comprehensive guide to jazz improvisation. Covers: scale choices • chord analysis • phrasing • melodies • harmonic progressions • more.
00695135 Book/CD Pack......................................$17.95

THE ART OF MODULATING
FOR PIANISTS AND JAZZ MUSICIANS
*by Carlos Salzedo &
Lucile Lawrence*
Schirmer
The Art of Modulating is a treatise originally intended for the harp, but this edition has been edited for use by intermediate keyboardists and other musicians who have an understanding of basic music theory. In its pages you will find: table of intervals; modulation rules; modulation formulas; examples of modulation; extensions and cadences; ten fragments of dances; five characteristic pieces; and more.
50490581 ....$19.99

BUILDING A JAZZ VOCABULARY
By Mike Steinel
A valuable resource for learning the basics of jazz from Mike Steinel of the University of North Texas. It covers: the basics of jazz • how to build effective solos • a comprehensive practice routine • and a jazz vocabulary of the masters.
00849911 ....$19.95

THE CYCLE OF FIFTHS
by Emile and Laura De Cosmo
This essential instruction book provides more than 450 exercises, including hundreds of melodic and rhythmic ideas. The book is designed to help improvisors master the cycle of fifths, one of the primary progressions in music. Guaranteed to refine technique, enhance improvisational fluency, and improve sight-reading!
00311114 ....$16.99

THE DIATONIC CYCLE
by Emile and Laura De Cosmo
Renowned jazz educators Emile and Laura De Cosmo provide more than 300 exercises to help improvisors tackle one of music's most common progressions: the diatonic cycle. This book is guaranteed to refine technique, enhance improvisational fluency, and improve sight-reading!
00311115 ....$16.95

EAR TRAINING
*by Keith Wyatt,
Carl Schroeder and Joe Elliott*
Musicians Institute Press
Covers: basic pitch matching • singing major and minor scales • identifying intervals • transcribing melodies and rhythm • identifying chords and progressions • seventh chords and the blues • modal interchange, chromaticism, modulation • and more.
00695198 Book/2-CD Pack $24.95

EXERCISES AND ETUDES FOR THE JAZZ INSTRUMENTALIST
by J.J. Johnson
Designed as study material and playable by any instrument, these pieces run the gamut of the jazz experience, featuring common and uncommon time signatures and keys, and styles from ballads to funk. They are progressively graded so that both beginners and professionals will be challenged by the demands of this wonderful music.
00842018 Bass Clef Edition $16.95
00842042 Treble Clef Edition $16.95

JAZZOLOGY
THE ENCYCLOPEDIA OF JAZZ THEORY FOR ALL MUSICIANS
*by Robert Rawlins and
Nor Eddine Bahha*
This comprehensive resource covers a variety of jazz topics, for beginners and pros of any instrument. The book serves as an encyclopedia for reference, a thorough methodology for the student, and a workbook for the classroom.
00311167 ....$19.99

JAZZ THEORY RESOURCES
by Bert Ligon
Houston Publishing, Inc.
This is a jazz theory text in two volumes. **Volume 1 includes**: review of basic theory • rhythm in jazz performance • triadic generalization • diatonic harmonic progressions and analysis • substitutions and turnarounds • and more. **Volume 2 includes**: modes and modal frameworks • quartal harmony • extended tertian structures and triadic superimposition • pentatonic applications • coloring "outside" the lines and beyond • and more.
00030458 Volume 1 ....$39.95
00030459 Volume 2 ....$29.95

JOY OF IMPROV
*by Dave Frank
and John Amaral*
This book/CD course on improvisation for all instruments and all styles will help players develop monster musical skills! Book One imparts a solid basis in technique, rhythm, chord theory, ear training and improv concepts. **Book Two** explores more advanced chord voicings, chord arranging techniques and more challenging blues and melodic lines. The CD can be used as a listening and play-along tool.
00220005 Book 1 – Book/CD Pack......................$27.99
00220006 Book 2 – Book/CD Pack......................$26.99

THE PATH TO JAZZ IMPROVISATION
by Emile and Laura De Cosmo
This fascinating jazz instruction book offers an innovative, scholarly approach to the art of improvisation. It includes in-depth analysis and lessons about: cycle of fifths • diatonic cycle • overtone series • pentatonic scale • harmonic and melodic minor scale • polytonal order of keys • blues and bebop scales • modes • and more.
00310904 ....$14.99

THE SOURCE
THE DICTIONARY OF CONTEMPORARY AND TRADITIONAL SCALES
by Steve Barta
This book serves as an informative guide for people who are looking for good, solid information regarding scales, chords, and how they work together. It provides right and left hand fingerings for scales, chords, and complete inversions. Includes over 20 different scales, each written in all 12 keys.
00240885 ....$18.99

21 BEBOP EXERCISES
by Steve Rawlins
This book/CD pack is both a warm-up collection and a manual for bebop phrasing. Its tasty and sophisticated exercises will help you develop your proficiency with jazz interpretation. It concentrates on practice in all twelve keys — moving higher by half-step — to help develop dexterity and range. The companion CD includes all of the exercises in 12 keys.
00315341 Book/CD Pack..................................$17.95

HAL•LEONARD® CORPORATION
7777 W. BLUEMOUND RD. P.O. BOX 13819 MILWAUKEE, WI 53213

Visit Hal Leonard online at
www.halleonard.com

Prices, contents & availability subject to change without notice.

0113